OVER THE DOOR

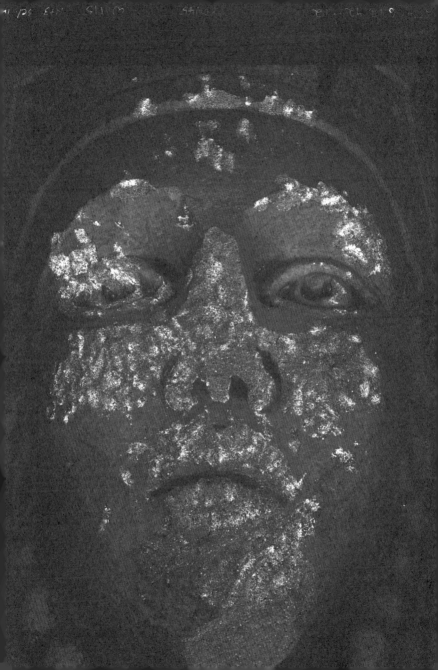

OVER THE DOOR

THE

ORNAMENTAL STONEWORK

OF NEW YORK

PHOTOGRAPHS BY JOHN YANG

1995
PRINCETON ARCHITECTURAL PRESS

Published by:
Princeton Architectural Press, Inc.
37 East 7th Street, New York, NY 10003
212.995.9620

Call 1.800.458.1131 for a free catalog of books

First Edition
Printed and bound in Canada by Friesen Printers
Typography by Naomi Yang

98 97 96 95   4 3 2 1

Excerpt from *Lectures and Conversations on Aesthetics, Psychology, and Religious Belief*, by Ludwig Wittgenstein, edited and translated by Cyril Barrett, ©1966 Basil Blackwell, courtesy University of California Press.
Excerpt from *Learning to Curse: Essays in Modern Culture*, by Stephen J. Greenblatt, ©1990 Routledge, Chapman & Hall, Inc.
Excerpt from *The Maintenance and Repair of Architectural Sandstone* ©1982 New York Landmarks Conservancy.

The publisher wishes to thank Caroline Green, Clare Jacobson, Therese Kelly, Mark Lamster, Bill Monaghan, Allison Saltzman, and Ann Urban of Princeton Architectural Press.

The photographer wishes to thank Kevin C. Lippert and Ann Urban of Princeton Architectural Press. He would also like to thank the New York Landmarks Conservancy for the permission to reproduce the excerpt from the above noted publication. The New York Landmarks Conservancy, located at 141 Fifth Avenue, New York, NY 10010, is a private not-for-profit organization that preserves and revitalizes buildings throughout the City and State of New York by providing grants, technical services, and public education programs. For further information call 212.995.5260.

ISBN 1-56898-057-4

Library of Congress Cataloging-in-Publication Data available from the publisher.

CONTENTS

INTRODUCTION

Architects have been forced by utility to construct certain bare structures and now the sculptor was called upon to assist in removing the repulsive features by decorative effects — a hard task.

— History of Architecture and the
Building Trades of Greater New York, 1899

The *"bare structures"* referred to were brownstone rowhouses and tenements built during the last decades of the 19th century, a period in which New York City experienced unprecedented growth.

The *"sculptors called upon to assist,"* were stoneworkers who emigrated from the British Isles and Northern Europe (30,000 by one account). They not only brought their craft — which they, like their forebears, practiced *in situ* — but, as evidenced by what they chose to depict, they also brought a fancy for the grotesque.

The *"decorative effects"* used *"in removing the repulsive features,"* were carvings that embellished the brownstone facades of the newly erected buildings. These consisted of both geometric articulations of architectural and structural elements, and figurative representations of human, animal, and plant forms — typically incongruously combined. In some instances, realistic depictions of men, women, and children — a few of whom were modeled after the original owners and occupants — created singular and compelling portraits. Their faces, heads, and busts, carved in the boldest of relief, adorned the keystones of arches over entrance doors.

What still remains of these *"decorative effects"* — as well as what has become of them — is what these photographs are about.

The 123 photographs included in this book were taken between October 1990 and November 1993. They were taken in New York City, in the borough of Manhattan, in its older residential neighborhoods, from the Lower East Side to Harlem.

Although ornamental stonework is the principal subject of these photographs, a few examples of other kinds of ornamentation are included, most notably the pressed-sheet metalwork that decorates the pediments crowning the facades of some houses.

I.

1.1

1.2

13

I.3

1.4

27

31

1.5

2.

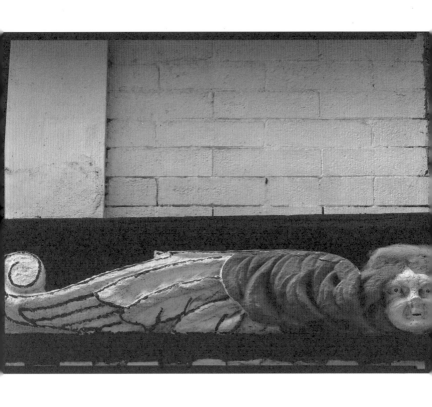

2.1

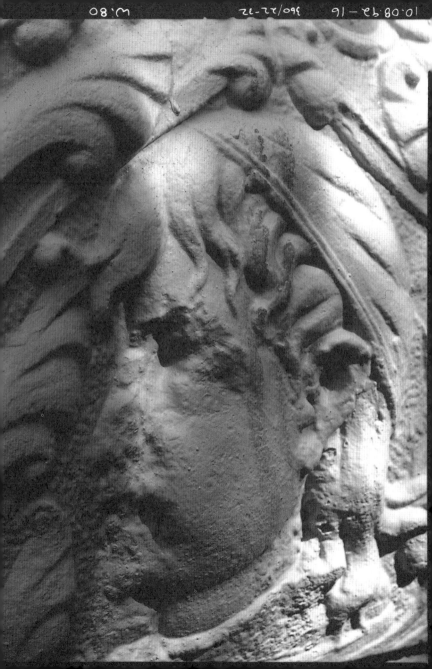

2.2

2.3

2.4

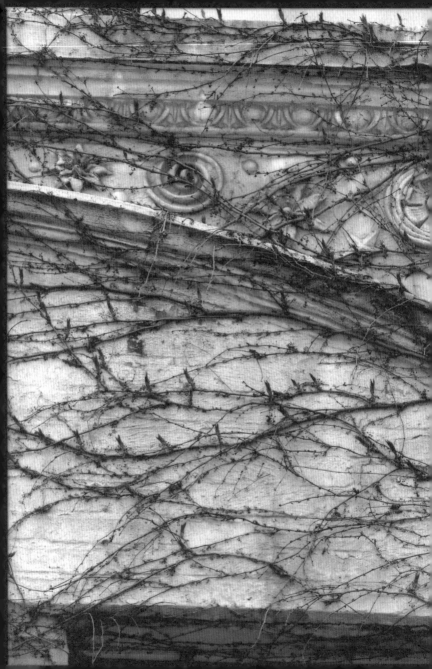

2.5

3.

3.1

3.2

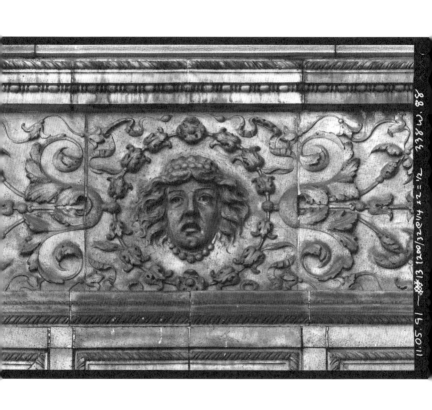

III

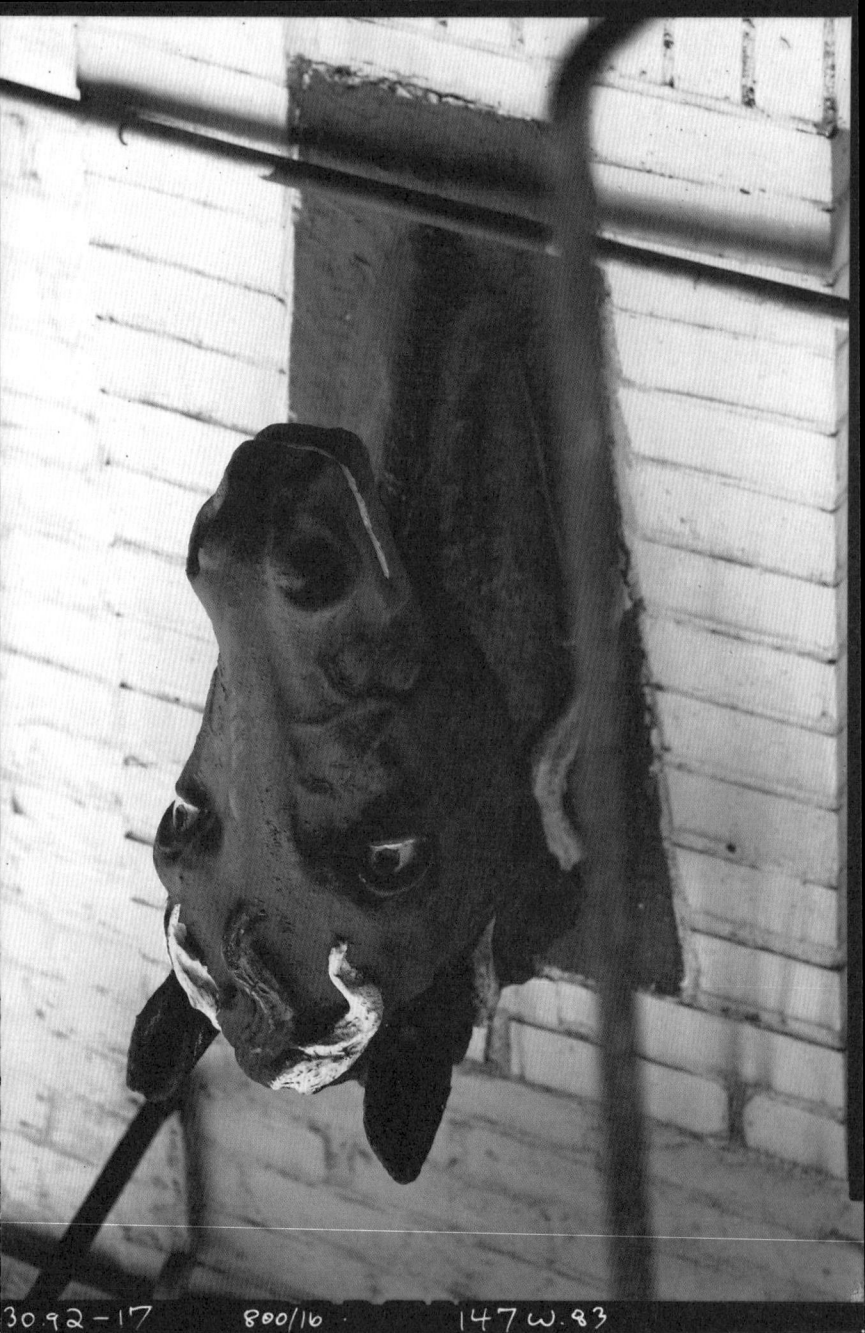

3·3

3·4

3·5

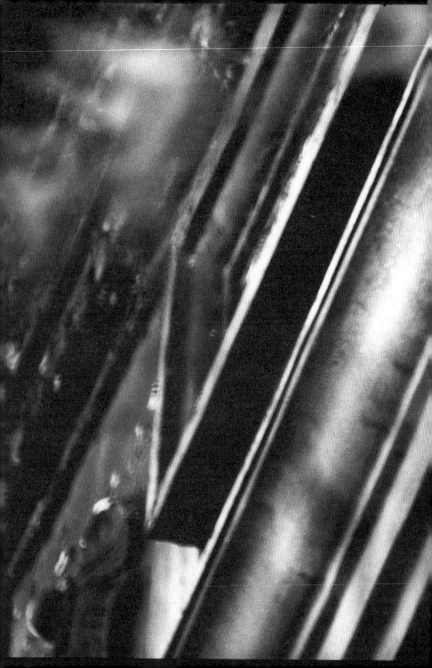

3.6

APPENDICES

1.

I draw a few dashes with a pencil and paper, and then ask: "Who is this?" and get the answer: "It is Napoleon." We have never been taught to call these marks, "Napoleon."

> LUDWIG WITTGENSTEIN
> *Lectures and Conversations,* 1966

2.

In the course of the foregoing remarks and throughout this volume, I have often felt much difficulty about the proper application of the terms, will, consciousness, and intention. Actions, which were at first voluntary, soon became habitual, and at last hereditary, and may then be performed even in opposition to the will. Although they often reveal the state of the mind, this result was not at first either intended or expected. Even such words as that "certain movements serve as a means of expression" are apt to mislead, as they imply that this was their primary purpose or object. This, however, seems rarely or never to have been the case; the movements having been at first either of some direct use, or the indirect effect of the excited state of the sensorium. An infant may scream either intentionally or instinctively to show that it wants food; but it has no wish or intention to draw its features into the peculiar form which so plainly indicates misery; yet some of the most characteristic expressions exhibited by man are derived from the act of screaming, as has been explained. . .

. . . But the question is, do our children acquire their knowledge of expression solely by experience through the power of association and reason?

As most of the movements of expression must have been gradually acquired, afterwards becoming instinctive, there seems to be some degree of *à priori* probability that their recognition would likewise have become instinctive. There is, at least, no greater difficulty in believing this than in admitting that, when a female quadruped first bears young, she knows the cry of distress of her offspring, or than in admitting that many animals instinctively recognize and fear their enemies; and of both these statements there can be no reasonable doubt. It is however extremely difficult to prove that our children instinctively recognize any expression. I attended to this point in my first-born infant, who could not have learnt anything by associating with other children, and I was convinced that he understood a smile and received pleasure from seeing one, answering it by another, at much too early an age to have learnt anything by experience. When this child was about four months old, I made in his presence many odd noises and strange grimaces, and tried to look savage; but the noises, if not too loud, as well as the grimaces, were all taken as good jokes; and I attributed this at the time to their being preceded or accompanied by smiles. When five months old, he seemed to understand a compassionate expression and tone of voice. When a few days over six months old, his nurse pretended to cry, and I saw that his face instantly assumed a melancholy expression, with the corners of the mouth strongly depressed; now this child could rarely have seen any other child crying, and never a grown-up person crying, and I should doubt whether at so early an age he could have reasoned on the subject. Therefore it seems to me that an innate feeling must have told him that the pretended crying of his nurse expressed grief; and

this through the instinct of sympathy excited grief in him.

M. Lemoine argues that, if man possessed an innate knowledge of expression, authors and artists would not have found it so difficult, as is notoriously the case, to describe and depict the characteristic signs of each particular state of mind. But this does not seem to me a valid argument. We may actually behold the expression changing in an unmistakable manner in a man or animal, and yet be quite unable, as I know from experience, to analyse the nature of the change. In the two photographs given by Duchenne of the same old man, almost every one recognized that the one represented a true, and the other a false smile; but I have found it very difficult to decide in what the whole amount of difference consists. It has often struck me as a curious fact that so many shades of expression are instantly recognized without any conscious process of analysis on our part. . .

CHARLES DARWIN
The Expression of the Emotions in Man and Animals, 1872

3.

I am fascinated by the signs of alteration, tampering, even destructiveness which many museums try to simply efface: first and most obviously, the act of displacement that is essential for the collection of virtually all older artifacts and most modern ones — pulled out of chapels, peeled off church walls, removed from decaying houses. . . Then too there are the marks on the artifacts themselves: the attempt to scratch out or deface the image of the devil in numerous late-medieval and Renaissance paintings, the concealing of the genitals in sculptured and painted figures, the iconoclastic smashing of human or divine representations, the evidence of cutting or reshaping to fit a new frame or purpose, the cracks or scorch marks or broken-off noses that indifferently record the grand disasters of history and the random accidents of trivial incompetence.

STEPHEN J. GREENBLATT
Learning to Curse, 1990

4.

APHORISM 31.
Restoration, so called, is the worst manner of Destruction.

Neither by the public, nor by those who have the care of public monuments, is the true meaning of the word *restoration* understood. It means the most total destruction which a building can suffer: a destruction out of which no remnants can be gathered: a destruction accompanied with false description of the thing destroyed. Do not let us deceive ourselves in this important matter; it is *impossible*, as impossible as to raise the dead, to restore anything that has ever been great or beautiful in architecture. That which I have above insisted upon as the life of the whole, that spirit which is given only by the hand and eye of the workman, never can be recalled. Another spirit may be given by another time, and it is then a new building; but the spirit of the dead workman cannot be summoned up, and commanded to direct other hands, and other thoughts. And as for direct and simple copying, it is palpably impossible. What copying can there be of surfaces that have been worn half an inch down? The whole finish of the work was in the half inch that is gone; if you attempt to restore that finish, you do it conjecturally; if you copy what is left, granting fidelity to be possible, (and what care, or watchfulness, or cost can secure it,) how is the new work better than the old? There was yet in the old *some* life, some mysterious suggestion of what it had been, and of what it had lost; some sweetness in the gentle lines which rain and sun had wrought. There can be none in the brute hardness of the new carving. Look at the animals which I have given in Plate 14., as an instance of living work, and suppose the markings of the scales and hair once worn away, of the wrinkles of the brows, and who shall ever restore them? The first step to restoration, (I have seen it, and that again and again — seen it on the Bapistery of Pisa, seen it on the Casa d'Oro at Venice, seen it on the Cathedral of Lisieux,) is to dash the old work to pieces; the second is usually to put up the cheapest and basest imitation which can escape detection, but in all cases, however careful, and however laboured, an imitation still, a cold model of such parts as *can* be modelled, with conjectural supplements; and my experience has as yet furnished me with only one instance, that of the Palais de Justice at Rouen, in which even this, the utmost degree of fidelity which is possible, has been attained, or even attempted.

Do not let us talk then of restoration. The thing is a Lie from beginning to end. You may make a model of a building as you may of a corpse, and your model may have the shell of the old walls within it as your cast might have the skeleton, with what advantage I neither see nor care: but the old building is destroyed, and that more totally and mercilessly than if it had sunk into a heap of dust, or melted into a mass of clay: more has been gleaned out of desolated Nineveh than ever will be out of re-built Milan.

APHORISM 30.
(The greatest glory is in its Age)

For, indeed, the greatest glory of a building is not in its stones, nor in its gold. Its glory is in its Age, and in that deep sense of voicefulness, of stern watching, of mysterious sympathy, nay, even of approval or condemnation, which we feel in walls that have long been washed by the passing waves of humanity. It is in their lasting witness against men, in their quiet contrast with the transitional character of all things, in the strength which, through the lapse of seasons and times, and the decline and birth of dynasties, and the changing of the face of the earth, and of the limits of the sea, maintains its sculptured shapeliness for a time insuperable, connects forgotten and following ages with each other, and half constitutes the identity, as it concentrates the sympathy, of nations: it is in that golden stain of time, that we are to look for the real light, and colour, and preciousness of architecture; and it is not until a building has assumed this character, till it has been entrusted with the fame, and hallowed by the deeds of men, till its walls have been witnesses of suffering, and its pillars rise out of the shadows of death, that its existence, more lasting as it is than that of the natural objects of the world around it, can be gifted with even so much as these possess, of language and of life.

JOHN RUSKIN
The Seven Lamps of Architecture, 1880

5.

ARCHITECTURAL SANDSTONE: HISTORY AND USE

Sandstone, particularly in its dark-colored brownstone form, is a significant material in the history of American building. "Brownstone" is the common name for the entire range of brown, red, purple, and pink sandstones widely used as building materials from the 1840's until the early 20th century. Most of the stone was quarried in Connecticut, Massachusetts, New Jersey, New York, and Pennsylvania.

Readily available and easily worked, brownstone found use as a building material as early as the 17th century in the northeastern United States. By the mid-19th century, writers such as Henry David Thoreau, painters such as Thomas Cole, and architects such as A.J. Davis were leading popular taste toward a romantic return to nature. Natural shapes, colors, and materials became especially valued in architecture; and brownstone, with its variety of surface textures and its rich, earth-toned color, emerged as a dominant American building material.

Thousands of urban row houses, as well as public and commercial buildings, churches, and mansions, were built with brownstone through the height of the material's popularity after the Civil War.

Almost as soon as sandstone became a prominent building material, it also became notorious for its tendency to decay. Now, more than one hundred years later, brownstone row houses and other sandstone buildings are popular again, and a new generation of owners faces the problem of sandstone decay. . .

LOOKING AT SANDSTONE: STRUCTURE

Sandstone has two basic structural characteristics.

1. It is made up of grains of sand and other mineral materials that are held together by natural cementing agents.

2. It has a layered structure. The grains that form it were deposited over centuries in layers, or strata, by water and the wind. Within the stone, natural zones of weakness called bedding planes occur where each layer comes into contact with the next. . .

DECAY OF SANDSTONE

The primary agent of stone deterioration is water. Contributing factors are likely to be the structure of the sandstone itself.

Water can cause stone decay in many ways: by eroding the surface; by carrying dissolved salts that later solidify, expand, and fracture the stone; by freezing inside the stone and popping the surface; and by causing the natural clay binder within the stone to swell. Waterborne pollutants can react chemically with the stone and form a hard crust that later fractures, or they can dissolve acid-sensitive binders in the stone, resulting in surface disintegration.

Sandstone's inherent structural character helps give rise to decay. Because sandstone is a sedimentary rock made, essentially, of sand and a cementing agent, the stone is porous and subject to failure both between the mineral grains

and along the bedding planes. Different types of cementing materials may make the stone susceptible to acid attack, clay swelling or mineral oxidation.

Even the best quality stone will suffer when improperly used. Historically, the most serious construction error has been the practice of face-bedding, or setting the stone with the bedding planes running vertically. Face-bedding allows water to penetrate along the bedding planes, weakening the bonds between the strata and causing the stone to separate and fall apart in layers.

Sometimes inferior or inappropriate stone was selected originally. Some sandstones are softer, weaker or less durable than others, and natural flaws may produce unsound stone even in a good quarry. Occasionally, freshly quarried stone was not given enough time to dry out before its natural water content froze in cold weather. This caused damage which could remain hidden until the stone was finished and in place. Poor design or construction of buildings can encourage water to collect and penetrate the stone, and poor repairs may also accelerate stone deterioration.

During the examination of a building, any or all of the following types of stone deterioration may be found.

Weathering. Disintegration of the stone's surface, most noticeable on tooled or carved stone. Usually caused by erosion, chemical action, and moisture freezing in the stone. Often the sand grains will rub off at the touch.

Exfoliation. Separation and loss of large areas of stone along the bedding planes. This occurs when the stone has been face-bedded, and it results in an uneven surface.

Blind Exfoliation. Separation of stone along bedding planes, but where the layers are still loosely attached behind the surface. This also results from face-bedding. The stone will sound hollow when lightly tapped with a rubber mallet.

Blistering. Swelling and rupturing of a thin uniform skin. This results from airborne chemicals reacting with the stone's surface, forming a hard, brittle skin. The blisters will often pop when touched.

Cracking. Narrow fractures from 1/16 to 1/2 inch wide.

Detachment. A clean break in the stone. This often results from a sharp impact, or from a concentration of stresses in a small area due to structural settlement.

NEW YORK LANDMARKS
CONSERVANCY
*The Maintenance and Repair
of Architectural Sandstone,* 1982

6.

TECHNICAL NOTES

Of the 123 photographs in this book, 14 were taken with a single-lens-reflex camera (Nikon F3HP) using lenses from 55 to 1000 mm. All others were taken with a 5" x 7" mono-rail view camera (Sinar Standard) fitted with a fifty-inch long custom-made bellows (Universal Bellows Co.). Most photographs were taken using telephoto lenses (Nikkor-T ED) with focal lengths of 600, 800, and 1200 mm. A 360 mm. wide-field apochromatic lens (Fujinon-A) was useful for close-ups. Two tripods (Gitzo 412 and 224) were needed to support the camera. Wind and vibration from traffic were recurrent problems. For this reason, a high-speed film with favorable reciprocity characteristics (Kodak T-MAX 400) was chosen to reduce exposure times. Film was tray-processed in a replenishment-type developer (Kodak T-MAX RS). Negatives were printed by contact on Palladio Paper and printing-out paper (Chicago Albumen Works).

Front Cover Photograph:
East 13th Street

First Six Photographs:

Last Six Photographs:

Back Cover Photograph:
West 75th Street